USAF STRIKE
AIRCRAFT

USAF STRIKE
AIRCRAFT

JOE CUPIDO

Published in 1991 by Osprey Publishing Limited
59 Grosvenor Street, London W1X 9DA

British Library Cataloguing in Publication Data

Cupido, Joe
    USAF strike aircraft
    I. Title
    623.7460973

ISBN 1855321769

Editor Dennis Baldry
Text Bill Gunston
Page design David Tarbutt
Printed in Hong Kong

Front cover General Dynamics
F-111A all-weather attack aircraft of
the 389th Tactical Fighter Training
Squadron, 366th Tactical Fighter
Wing, take the scenic route back to
Mountain Home AFB, Idaho. Both
Aardvarks are equipped with
underwing multiple ejector racks
(MERs), each of which is capable of
carrying six bombs in the Mk 82 class

Title page The Lockheed F-117A,
first stealth aircraft to go into service,
has an exterior made up of dozens of
flat reflective facets. The result is like
something from another world

Back cover McDonnell Douglas
F-15E Strike Eagles of the 405th
Tactical Fighter Wing taxi out for
take-off as Luke AFB bakes in
Arizona sunshine. Although
dedicated to 'mud-moving', once the
Strike Eagle has expended its air-to-
ground ordnance, it regains the
awesome manoeuvrability of the
F-15C/D fighter versions

Right The McDonnell Douglas F-4G is th
latest variant of the Phantom II. It has
electronic antennas below the nose
and above the tail

For a catalogue of all books published by Osprey Aerospace
please write to:

**The Marketing Department,
Octopus Illustrated Books, 1st Floor, Michelin House,
81 Fulham Road, London SW3 6RB**

Introduction

The Gulf War demonstrated air power in a way that — with the possible exception of the Israeli Three-day War in 1967 — has not been seen since World War 2. For once, an entire campaign was planned meticulously, without political interference, and carried through in textbook fashion. To say that strike aircraft — aircraft directed against tactical ground targets — made it possible to win the entire ground campaign in 100 hours, and with amazingly light casualties, is to state what is self-evident.

For many years until 1991 various influential people around the world, and most notably in Washington, had criticized modern airpower as something astronomically expensive that, in practice, would fail to work. These critics have now been so convincingly proved wrong that little will be heard from them until at least the next century. Of course, modern strike aircraft have to have powerful jet engines to thrust, powerful wings to lift, and strong pylons to carry ordnance. But what makes such aircraft so terribly effective is something far less obvious: avionics.

For a start, avionics enable modern aircraft to keep a round-the-clock watch on the enemy, in the uttermost detail. Thus, the attack airpower can be tasked with absolute precision. In World War 2 a British Typhoon pilot happened to see a German tank through a small gap in cloud cover. As a result by evening the 2nd SS Panzer Division ceased to exist — by sheer chance. In today's war chance is eliminated. Avionics finds and pinpoints every target. Avionics enables the strike aircraft to fly at almost ground level, under enemy radars, day or night, whilst navigating with unfailing accuracy over the entire flight plan (which can be complex, and, for example, include air refuelling). At the target, avionics makes certain that every weapon hits.

Avionics also plays a crucial role in the support aircraft which help to defeat the enemy's air defences. Such complicated aircraft as the EF-111A and F-4G exist solely in order to carry specialized avionics into the sky. The former does not even carry armament; its weapons are powerful electronic jammers. The F-4G's weapons are directed automatically against the enemy's radars, enabling accompanying strike aircraft to reach their targets unscathed.

Today there is a new sort of strike aircraft that relies not upon brute-force electronic jamming but upon its near-invisibility to enemy defence systems. The strange-looking Lockheed F-117A heralds a new age in air warfare in which bombs suddenly arrive from what seems to be a clear sky. This idea was singled out for especial attack by the 'expert critics'. Never was any new weapon so convincingly demonstrated as the black Stealth Fighter over difficult point targets in Iraq.

Two of the most significant warplanes of modern times wait side-by-side at Edwards AFB, destined to be refurbished and put into the USAF Flight Test Center Museum. Left, 63-9766, the first prototype F-111A. Right, 74-159, the second prototype B-1A strategic bomber

Contents

Strike Eagle

Above An F-15E passes straight overhead, showing weapons ejector racks fitted. The huge wing, of 608 sq ft, relies simply on its size to give the F-15E powerful manoeuvrability, even at weights around 40 tons. It has simple plain flaps and a fixed leading edge. In theory a large wing is undesirable for high speed at low level, but nobody has told the Strike Eagle about this!

Right Inlets down and flaps at the takeoff setting, 86-0184, the second F-15E, sets out on another mission at Edwards with the F-15 CTF (Combined Test Force)

The No 2 aircraft heads for the Edwards runway, without ordnance but carrying the two LANTIRN pods. These avionics additions enable terrifyingly low missions to be flown on the blackest night

Distinguished by its F-15E titles and fin art, 86-0183 was the first of the multi-role E models to come off the line at St Louis. Unlike 71-291, the original prototype (converted from the No 2 F-15B) which was two-tone dark green, production aircraft are grey

A scene on the flight line at Luke
AFB, Arizona. Here the 405th
Tactical Fighter Wing carries out the
whole F-15E flight crew training
programme. Every pilot posted here
is experienced in air/air or
air/ground. Now they have to learn
to be good at both, and to work in
close partnership with a backseater

Preceding pages Training at Luke involves every aspect of flying the E, including dropping bombs and air/air and air/ground gunnery. The muzzle of the M61 gun is the black rectangle between the inlet and the wing. Under the wing is a Sidewinder, and Snakeye retarded bombs are loaded under the fuselage

Signing acceptance of the aircraft — usually just confirmation that there is a signature against every ground-crew task — is one of the key items in the preflight walkaround. Usually bombs and missiles (such as this Sidewinder) are readied for use after taxiing to the runup area

The crew chief assists the crew run
through cockpit checks. Then, the
long ladder removed, the pilot calls
'Arms in ?' to the backseater before
closing the huge canopy, which
powers gently down and then slides
forward to lock with a clunk and
pressure-seal the cockpit

Left Martin Marietta's LANTIRN pods play a crucial role in missions at night. Under the left inlet is the target pod, containing two sensors, a FLIR (forward-looking infrared) and laser, boresighted together and slewable to keep 'looking' at the target, for example to designate smart bombs. On the far side is the navigation pod, housing a TFR (terrain-following radar) and a second FLIR with fixed imagery

Below left Head-on one gets an idea of the bulge added by the CFT (conformal fuel tank), one of which is scabbed on each side (but it can be removed). Each 'Dash-4' CFT has a capacity of 9100 lb (4128 kg), or about 624 gal (750 US gal), and adds hardly any drag. Note the inlet in the UP position, which is normal with the engines shut down. Under the inlet is a LANTIRN pod

Below Instead of the standard tail this aircraft carries the title of the Luke training unit, the 405th TFW. Flying is intensive, and as well as passing out crews further work was needed to back up Edwards in investigating the carriage and release of many kinds of weapon. Here the load is dummy Snakeyes and Sidewinders

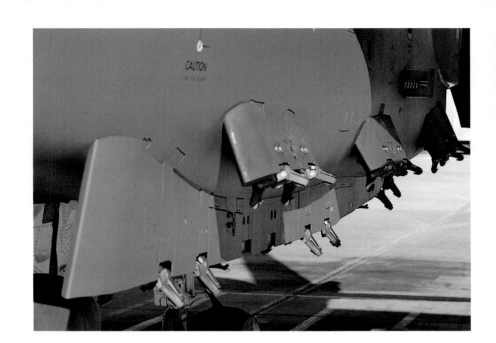

Left The E can carry an amazing 24,500 lb of ordnance. This makes it hard to believe that when the F-15 was young the Air Force was adamant that it should never be 'compromised' by having to fly strike missions, and coined the slogan 'Not a pound for air to ground!' Completely new tangential ejector release units project from the CFTs, six along each side, without affecting the triple carriers on the wing and centreline stations. The wing pylons can carry Mavericks, as well as AAMs

Below left Taxiing out, one gets a rear view of the closed nozzles. Early Es have the same Pratt & Whitney F100-220 as the F-15C, but the engine bay has been designed to accept either the new F100-229 or the rival General Electric F110-129. Either boosts thrust per engine from 23,450 lb to the 29,000 lb level, but the new engines are heavier and need ballast to be added in the nose

Below When the tangential stores carriers are not fitted the E looks very much like earlier F-15s, though of course it always has a bigger canopy to cover both cockpits. Among many other structural changes the windscreen and canopy have been cleared to withstand a low-centre birdstrike at 500 knots. On the centreline here is a 508-gal (610-US gal) drop tank. This tank alone would have filled six Battle of Britain Spitfires

Preceding pages Three of a section of four aircraft about to depart from Luke on a local training mission. Two had Mk 82 Snakeye 500-lb retarded bombs and AIM-9 Sidewinders, while the other two had inert training versions of the same weapons

Below This aircraft bears the tail code of the wing (with TAC badge), and on the left inlet the badges of the wing and its constituent squadrons. The giant radome over the impressive new APG-70 multi-mode radar is almost the same low-vis colour as the rest of the aircraft

An F-15E about to open up for takeoff from Luke AFB. Not very obvious is the fact that the entire structure of these aircraft had to be redesigned to withstand a far more severe life, pulling 9G at low levels and living in turbulent air at weights up to a staggering 81,000 lb (36,741 kg). The maximum takeoff weight of the original F-15A interceptor was less than half as much!

Right Looking starkly warlike — which it certainly is — this F-15E is on the strength of the first fully operational combat unit, the 4th TFW, at Seymour-Johnson AFB, North Carolina. This wing's 336th TFS was declared operational in October 1989. The 4th TFW sent 26 aircraft to the Gulf in 1990

Below The engines go to MIL power and then smoothly into afterburner (the further aircraft), the nozzles simultaneously opening fully. Here all the weight is still on the landing gears, which have strengthened legs and bigger radial tyres (compared with an F-15C) to handle the higher weights

Left Tail-on, this aircraft of the 4th TFW (tail code SJ) shows that the jet nozzles are close together and the fins truly vertical, unlike several other modern fighters. The tip of the left fin carries the aft RWR (radar warning receiver) on top, plus the left ECM and tail nav light. The right fin carries front and rear ECM antennas and the anti-collision light. The high-power aft ECM antenna is just inboard of the right tailplane (it can be seen in the plan view on page 8)

Boomer's eye view of an F-15E from Luke waiting its turn. The boom receptacle, here still closed, is outlined in white immediately inboard of the left wing leading edge. Around the wingtip are the forward ECM antenna, nav light and electroluminescent panel to aid formation flying

Aardvark and Raven

Left An epoch-making and often controversial aircraft, the F-111 nevertheless introduced the world to the concept of low-level terrain-following through mountains at night, followed by a blind first-pass attack on a point target. One of the controversial ideas was to seat the crew side-by-side — and in an ejectable capsule!

Above The EF-111A Raven is a total rebuild by Grumman of the General Dynamics F-111A attack aircraft. What emerged was a far more costly aircraft, painted grey, which carried no weapons except highly capable receivers and, in a 'canoe pod' underneath, a row of powerful jammers. It can serve as a stand-off jammer protecting friendly airspace, or it can accompany attack aircraft on missions over enemy territory, jamming hostile radars and communications. This EF serves with the 366th TFW's 39th ECS (Electronic Combat Sqn) at Mountain Home AFB, Idaho

Overleaf At first glance the shape and colour of the EF-111A might also be mistaken for the far larger Soviet Tu-160. But the giant SIR (system integrated receiver) pod on the fin is absolutely distinctive. With this the EF picks up everything the enemy might transmit, on all wavebands. There is even an IR heat receiver facing aft

Though the left/right upward hinged canopies were unchanged, the EF cockpit is utterly unlike that of other F-111s. In particular the right half is configured for an Electronic Warfare Officer instead of a Weapon System Officer. Small pylons above the wing gloves carry the ALQ-137 receiver and ALR-62 forward radar warning receiver

One thing that didn't change is that lowering the wing slats, rotating glove or flaps reveals bright red painted inner structure. One each side of the fin are ALQ-99 Band 1 and Band 2 antennas. This EF is in the front-line with the 42nd ECS at RAF Upper Heyford, Oxfordshire, England

Overleaf The most colourful F-111 flying today is probably USAF No 67-0159. Built as the first long-span FB-111A, it is today flying from McClellan AFB, California, as the unique improvement testbed for all modifications to F-111 fleet aircraft. The vast majority of the significant changes have been avionics updates

Another Raven outside its HAS (hardened aircraft shelter) at RAF Upper Heyford. It is coupled up to the towing system which pulls it into the shelter backwards, so that it is facing the right way to come out in a hurry. The 42nd played a major role in Desert Storm in early 1991

Below Coming in to land at Upper Heyford, the F-111E of the Commander of the 20th Tactical Fighter Wing displays the colourful tail stripe used by F-84s of the 20th some 40 years earlier. The E model was the first to have the larger and more efficient Triple Plow II inlets, though the engine remained the original Pratt & Whitney TF30-3

Bottom right This E of the 20th TFW shows a common but odd mixture of thrust and drag, with the giant barn-door of a landing-gear door (which also serves as the speed brake) fully extended, with the engines in full afterburner! Under the wings are practice-bomb carriers and outboard ejector-release units for Mk 82 bombs, put down on ranges in Scotland and Spain. Under the rear fuselage can be seen the ALQ-131 electronic jammer pod

Right Even a local training sortie requires the pilot and WSO to bring aboard a heavy load of kit. And that's without needing parachutes, because emergency escape is taken care of by the capsule. On this occasion at Upper Heyford they walked to their aircraft.

Right Taxiing along the centreline, with canopies open and wings and gloves in the high-lift regime. The E needs the high-lift features, because on a maximum-weight takeoff its thrust/weight ratio is only 0.4

Left In contrast, the F-111F has the somewhat better thrust/weight ratio of 0.502. Another advance in the F is the addition of the Pave Tack belly pod, which includes a laser for designating targets for the GBU-16B/B smart bomb of the Paveway II series. Based on the Mk 83 bomb (nominal 1000 lb), it proved its precision in Libya and Iraq

Below On the ground a 'One-Eleven' usually looks like an ungainly waddling duck, further encumbered by the giant belly door hanging half-open. This E is heading for the Upper Heyford runway carrying dispensers which, at the practice range, each dispense up to six small bomblets, one on each run. They hit with a shotgun-shell marking charge so that accuracy can be assessed

Preceding pages Mirage refractions off the taxiway at RAF Lakenheath distort the appearance of the second of a pair of F-111Fs of the 48th TFW. They are carrying Mk 84 2000 lb bombs as well as the practice dispensers. Pave Tacks are rotated to lie inside the fuselage except when near the target

Left With most Aardvarks, when the pilot rocks the power levers right forward into 'burner' at the start of the takeoff, not a lot happens. With the F the acceleration is significantly more positive, especially when the only external load is two practice dispensers

Below left Bright shock diamonds stream out behind the Pratt & Whitney TF30-100 afterburning turbofans as F-111F 74-177 accelerates down Lakenheath's 9000 ft runway. Lightly loaded this F should be airborne in much less than 2000 ft

Below The pilot hauls back at 140 knots, the broad tailerons rotate nose-down pushing down the tail, and the nose points up towards the sky. Aardvarks have done this perhaps one million times. Soon this F will tuck the ungainly gear away and look more purposeful

At Cannon AFB, New Mexico, the 27th TFW flies the F-111D, a costly variant which originally had so-called Mk II avionics unlike those of any other version. Here munitions personnel prepare to load a 2000 lb Mk 84 bomb on 68-136

49

With bombs in the class of the Mk 84 you want to do everything right first time. Like other versions the F-111D has in recent years undergone a total gutting and replacement of its avionics, though in today's harsh climate its future front-line life may be short

The official line is that side-by-side seating improves co-ordination between the pilot (on the left) and WSO; but many Aardvark crews would say the arrangement is not particularly popular. Most pilots would rather have a backseater than a rightseater, and every tactical pilot would far prefer a good all-round view

Below Among the F-111D's other non-standard features are the TF30-9 engine, slightly more powerful than the Dash-3 engine at 19,600 lb, and a 20-mm M61 gun with a drum housing 2084 rounds inside the forward part of the weapon bay. The gun's presence is betrayed by the slightly deeper fuselage bottom line aft of the nose gear

Right Here FB-111A 69-6508 is seen in 1990, wearing a totally different colour scheme and, sadly, no longer in front-line service. At that time the intention was to convert these still eminently usable aircraft for conventional tactical missions, with the designation F-111G, and assign them to airfields in the United Kingdom. By 1991 the harsh decision had been taken to restrict USAF front-line strength wherever possible to multi-role aircraft. So, F-15E and F-16C/A-16 yes, F-111G no

Below USAF No 69-6514 was the very last FB-111A built for Strategic Air Command. Here, showing plenty of red structure, it taxies out in 1984 when it was fully operational in the nuclear role. In 1990, just 20 years after its entry to service, the FB force was deactivated.

Preceding pages Some people might think of better assignments than Cannon, out in the desert near the town of Clovis, but the weather is usually perfect – which is just what you don't want when training crews to fight in places where the weather is terrible. Here an Aardvark of the 27th waits for its crew in the brilliant sunlight. The horizontal tailerons normally rotate to this angle as hydraulic pressure runs down after stopping engines

FB-111As are still being converted into F-111Gs at Sacramento Air Logistics Center, and the intention is to add them to the updated 'digitized' D-models of the 27th TFW at Cannon AFB. They retain SRAM capability, and will be equipped to fire the AGM-131A SRAM II

57

Left Boomer's view of an F-111G, alias modified FB-111A, in 1989. Most F-111 versions are cleared to refuel in flight to well beyond MTO (maximum take-off) weight, such as 100,000 lb instead of 92,500. The FB-111A, however, was always cleared to a single maximum weight of 114,300 lb

Right Because of its increased weights the FB-111A was fitted with a wing of increased span. In the 72.5° maximum-sweep position the wings extend beyond the horizontal tails, whereas in tactical F-111s they stop well short. Less obvious is the fact that the landing gears were strengthened

F-111As of Tactical Air Command seen in 1982 from the boomer's position in a KC-135 of the Utah Air National Guard. When it was a new type in service the 'One Eleven' gained a reputation for needing less back-up from other aircraft – tankers and electronic jammers, for example – than any other aircraft. Even today its internal fuel capacity is exceptional for a 'fighter type' aircraft, and any member of the species can cross the Atlantic non-stop without tanker support

Overleaf Scenically beautiful, but no place for a forced landing, rugged hills unroll past three Aardvarks during a practice air refuelling mission in 1983. Of course, a refuelling is always performed with wings at $16°$

Stealth fighter

Left An aerodynamicist might be forgiven for wondering how the Lockheed F-117A manages to fly. Never before had the shape of an aircraft been so completely dictated by non-aerodynamic factors, in this case the reflectivity of the external skin to radar illumination from somewhere in front of the aircraft. Head-on one can also see the vital FLIR (forward-looking infrared) ball ahead of the windscreen. This shows the pilot the target and is slaved to a DLIR (downward-looking infrared) under the nose which designates the target for a smart bomb

Below The massive canopy would have to be jettisoned before ejecting. The frame, like all the rest of the external skin, has zigzag edges parallel with the diagonal lines of the wings and tail. To avoid potentially large radar echoes from inside the cockpit the transparent areas have special coatings. The very pinnacle of the aircraft contains a floodlight which faces aft to illuminate the boom receptacle during air refuelling

COL AL WHITLEY

Preceding pages Like its ancestor the SR-71A 'Blackbird' the F-117A is housed in individual hangars, or 'barns'. Here seen from inside its hangar at TTR (Tonopah Test Range) this view of a 117 with USAF personnel to give scale shows that it is actually quite a large aircraft. Despite the sharp sweep the span is 43 ft 4 in, and length 63 ft 11 in — both values almost exactly the same as for the F-15. The huge inboard and outboard elevons droop naturally when hydraulic pressure is absent

Below When the weird Lockheed was highly secret the 4450th Tactical Group were exhausted by having to do all their flying at night. Today there is no problem, and (redesignated as the 37th Tactical Fighter Wing) the Tonopah unit can pull its strange birds out into the sunshine. In 1990 the 59 production aircraft still exhibited some visible differences, notably to the engine inlets. By 1991 all had probably been brought up to the latest standard

Right A major design feature of the F-117A is its sharp leading edge and completely flat undersurface. Unlike all other recent aircraft the wing does not have a smoothly curved aerofoil profile but is made up of flat panels joined along sharp edges. Ben Rich, head of the design team at Lockheed's famed Skunk Works, says, 'The trick is to make all the sharp angles and flow breakaways help each other. Like that the airplane can actually fly'. The maximum speed of the F-117A is probably in the region of 0.85 Mach

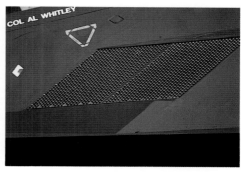

Above Almost the entire exterior of the F-117A is covered with RAM (radar-absorbent materials). Two places where the RAM has to be compromised are the canopy and the engine air inlets. At least, as this is a subsonic aircraft, the inlet can be of large area and fixed geometry. The inlet has the form of a giant rectangle divided into two squares, leaning backwards and outwards. The face of each square is covered by a grid, each element of which is a faceted RAM knife-edge. The edges are closer together than likely enemy radar wavelengths, so (in theory) all the energy striking the inlet is reflected in the desired direction. Prolonged efforts were needed to overcome problems with icing (birdstrikes are still annoying), and on takeoff additional air is sucked in through a large door above the inlet duct

The 59th and last F-117A was handed over to the Air Force at a ceremony at Lockheed's Palmdale assembly plant on 12 July 1990. Prominent here, the landing gears were among many items where some off-the-shelf parts (designed for other aircraft) were used to reduce cost. The leading edges are sharp, straight and swept at exactly $67.5°$. Around the apex are no fewer than four air-data probes, each ending in a four-sided pointed pyramid with a small hole in each face — 16 holes in all. Close beside the nose gear, on the starboard side, can be seen the large DLIR window — instrumental in putting a bomb within inches of the aiming point on the Ministry of Defence in Baghdad

The massive canopy is powered up by a large ram, and incorporates exceptionally powerful explosive jettison devices. The HUD (head-up display) is of modified F/A-18 Hornet type. Ground crew wear special footwear, and overalls proclaiming INTAKES ONLY

Right Not least of the strange features of the F-117A is the tail. The twin all-moving rudders, used for yaw only, lean sharply back at the same 67.5° angle as the wing, and in the same way have an extraordinary profile made of absolutely flat panels. One F-117A lost a rudder during extreme testing and came back safely. Some aircraft have carried the TAC badge, some (as here) the wing identity and others that of the squadron

Left From the tip one can see the amazing 'non-aerodynamic' profile of the wing, dictated purely by radar-reflective considerations. The giant elevons, which hang down until the engines are started, provide all control in pitch and roll. Driven by power units controlled by a quad-redundant FBW (fly by wire) system, they make this strange bird very nice to fly. Some people were misled by its nickname of Wobblin Goblin and thought it must be a real handful (it is not)

Far left Minimizing the radar, infrared and aural signature from the engines was another of the giant problems. Each General Electric F404-F1D2 turbofan, basically the same as the F/A-18 Hornet engine but without an afterburner, puts out about 10,800 lb thrust. A large flow of cool air is induced by a mixer around the engine nozzle, cooling and slowing down the resultant jet. This jet issues from unique flat slit nozzles along the trailing edge. The lower lip, protected by quartz tiles so that it stays quite cool and retains its precise shape, projects further back and also curves up, so that from this angle the actual nozzle cannot be seen. A red tag hangs from the arrester hook

Right All F-117A drivers wear appropriate shoulder patches. The 415th Tactical Fighter Squadron, 'Nightstalkers', is one of the three squadrons making up the only 'stealth' unit in the world at present, the 37th TFW. One of its aircraft (No 790, believed to be 80-790) was picked to go on show at Nellis

Below Though photographs had been seen previously, the real breakthrough for aviation buffs, and the general public, came on 21 April 1990 when two aircraft from the 37th TFW were flown to a crowded Nellis AFB and parked on the ramp. Red nylon cords kept visitors from actually touching the aircraft. This one is being towed to the parking spot

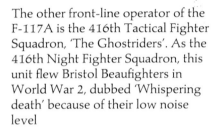

The other front-line operator of the F-117A is the 416th Tactical Fighter Squadron, 'The Ghostriders'. As the 416th Night Fighter Squadron, this unit flew Bristol Beaufighters in World War 2, dubbed 'Whispering death' because of their low noise level

Conversion on to the F-117A is handled by the 417th Tactical Fighter Training Squadron. 'The Bandits'. So far every pilot to go through the course has been an already experienced tactical pilot, with hundreds of hours at low level at night or in adverse weather. There is still much to learn, and as most pupils previously flew F-111s they now have to learn to fly the mission alone

All three squadrons together, with their associated maintenance and air base units, make up the 37th Tactical Fighter Wing, the elite unit which is the only one in the world to have gone to war with stealth aircraft. Formerly the 4450th Tactical Group, formed in 1980, the 37th is scheduled soon to move to a better-equipped home, Holloman AFB, New Mexico

On landing it is routine to stream the braking parachute, which is circular, very large and usually black (sometimes white). Its size reflects the high arrival speed, partly because of the inefficient aerofoil profile (with no high-lift devices) and partly the fact that Tonopah is one of the most 'hot and high' airfields in the United States

With cancellation of the A-12A Avenger, the F-117A is the only modern tactical strike aircraft available to US forces. All others are vulnerable 'high observability' designs. With a total force level below 50 aircraft, the ability of the United States to attack high-value targets of a sophisticated enemy will be painfully limited until, at the earliest, the end of the century

Wild Weasel

One of the world's classic combat aircraft designs, the McDonnell Phantom II was designed as the AH-1 multi-role carrier-based attack aircraft, modified and put into production as the F4H (F-4B) carrier-based interceptor and then modified into the land-based F-4C attack fighter and RF-4C multi-sensor reconnaissance aircraft. The final version is the F-4G Wild Weasel SAM killer, dedicated to detecting and knocking out the radars that guide enemy surface-to-air missiles

Overleaf The F-4G entered service with the 35th Tactical Fighter Wing, with tail code WW, from Wild Weasel. Later this code passed to the 37th TFW, at George AFB, California, with whom this aircraft was flying in 1986. As noted earlier, in October 1989 the 37th became the unique unit flying the F-117A

Right This F-4G was departing from George in September 1989 in the configuration for a long flight, even an overseas deployment. Three external tanks give a range of about 2300 miles without air refuelling. The gold stripe across the fin is one of the electroluminescent strips to aid formation flying by night

Below right The F-4Gs were modified to carry an F-15 type tank of 500 gal (600 US gal) capacity on the centreline. This example, 69-292, was seen in June 1986 at George AFB about to fly a local sortie carrying an AGM-65A Maverick air/ground missile. At that time the paint scheme was Europe I green

Below The first Wild Weasel aircraft were two-seat F-100F Super Sabres in Vietnam. They were replaced by a far better-equipped aircraft, the two-seat Republic F-105G Thunderchief. A notable feature of this, the final version of 'the Thud', was that its jammer pods were scabbed on flush against each side of the fuselage. They equipped the 37th TFW at George AFB, but this one was photographed in June 1974 at McClellan AFB

Right Today the Phantoms are painted in low-visibility grey, with toned-down markings. Instead of having a giant black nose radome only the tip of the nose is black, though there is a dark panel ahead of the windscreen. This F-4G was returning to George AFB, near Victorville, California, in 1988. It was obviously a long cross-country flight because the aircraft is carrying a Travel Pod housing the crew's luggage

Below The chief sensor of the F-4G is the APR-38 radar homing and warning system. It requires no fewer than 52 additional antennas to be added all round the aircraft, of which the biggest are a metal tubular pod on top of the fin and this much larger glassfibre pod under the nose. The undernose pod required removal of the internal M61 20 mm gun

Left Apart from self-homing HARM and Shrike anti-radar missiles the Wild Weasels also often carried EO (electro-optical) guided bombs or, especially, CBUs (cluster bomb units), such as the CBU-52 and -58. They mean to place all their ordnance directly on target, so it is surprising to find this aircraft about to fly a mission with two triplets of Mk 82 500 lb GP bombs. Another unusual feature is that the central splitter plate has been removed from the ram-air inlet at the base of the fin

Below Photographed in 1986, this F-4G was one of a number fitted with a large optical-camera system in the right forward missile bay. It is also carrying an AGM-88 HARM on the left pylon. To avoid blinding the Bear (the backseater) during operation of the camera system his canopy was modified with transparent panes

Right The AGM-88A HARM (High-speed Anti-Radar Missile) is the most important weapon carried by the F-4G. A product of Texas Instruments, it weighs about 796 lb at launch and flies at over Mach 2, homing automatically on to enemy radars up to 11 miles away. Its main drawback is its size and weight. The British Alarm does an even more versatile job (itself hovering to seek out the biggest threat) but is so much smaller a Tornado can carry nine. Unlike HARM, Alarm has a 100% record in action, but both did a good job in the Gulf

Below right McDonnell Aircraft built 1405 F-4Es, starting with a fixed but blown leading edge in 1966 and ending with a slatted wing in 1978. To produce the F-4Gs 116 F-4Es were carefully picked from Blocks 42 through 45, all funded in 1969. All had the slatted wing and a good airframe fatigue index. They were rebuilt by USAF Ogden (Utah) Air Logistic Center. From a distance a G looks much like an E, were it not for the fin-cap antenna and, in this case, the HARM missile

Left As an alternative to HARM, Wild Weasels can carry AGM-45 Shrike. This was based mainly on the airframe of the AIM-7 Sparrow air-to-air missile, though the tail is visibly different. Shrikes are shorter and slimmer than HARM, launch weight being about 390 lb. Early versions in the Vietnam war were disappointing, often failing to work, but prolonged development through many versions resulted in receivers and guidance systems with an acceptable chance of homing on to radars of particular wavelengths

Left Taking off from George AFB on a local training mission this F-4G is carrying a Westinghouse ALQ-119 ECM (electronic countermeasures) jammer pod under the left forward missile bay. One of the oldest ECM pods in service, ALQ-119 exists in many versions, often visibly different from the addition of extra gondola sections underneath. This example is ALQ-119(V)-15, also seen on page 82. A bigger ALQ-119 is seen on page 92

Below After 20 years the F-4G Wild Weasels are still very much in the front line. This example flies with the 480th Tactical Fighter Squadron, at Spangdahlem AB in Germany, alongside the 52nd TFW. Wild Weasels from here played a central role in the Desert Storm war in the Gulf

Overleaf A pleasing study of an F-4G on a training mission over Germany from Spangdahlem. It is carrying self-defence AIM-9P Sidewinders, as well as a long-gondola version of the ALQ-119 jammer pod, painted grey to match the aircraft. Some pods are dark green, and all were originally white

Strato-fortress

A legend in its own lifetime, the BUFF (politely rendered as big ugly fat fella) has a service record without parallel. Designed to drop a nuclear weapon from the thin stratosphere, it did that job for ten years before entering the much harsher world of low-level operations, and not with one bomb but with hundreds. For 40 years the B-52 has become structurally stronger, better in systems and propulsion, adapted to new weapons and, above all, more capable in offensive and defensive avionics. Yet this B-52G looks very much like the first B-52A of 38 years ago

Below A B-52G rumbles along the taxiway at Tinker AFB, Oklahoma. The B-52's slewable (20° left/right) four twin-wheel landing trucks enable landings to be made in crosswinds up to 45 knots blowing 90° to the runway

Left After initially being somewhat cool about the use of nose art on its aircraft, Strategic Air Command now recognizes the positive contribution that this traditional practice makes to the morale of air and ground crews. Much of the nose art and names worn by B-52s today were originally applied to B-17s and B-24s during World War 2, and this fact is usually acknowledged on the aircraft concerned. Interestingly, *Damage Inc* is signed by the artist – 'Cooke '89'; *Eternal Guardian* sums up the alert status of the nuclear-armed B-52s which continue to form a large part of SAC's offensive capability

Left The introduction of the General Dynamics AGM-86B air-launched cruise missile (ALCM) gave the B-52 a formidable and flexible stand-off strike/attack capability. A total of twelve ALCMs are carried in tandem triplets on a pair of substantial wing pylons. Alternatively, the pylons can accept four GD AGM-109H MRASMs (Medium Range Air-to-Surfaces Missiles). This variant of the Tomahawk cruise missile dispenses large conventional submunitions and is especially suitable for use against airbases

Below left If no external stores are carried, the B-52G is capable of 595 mph (925 km/h) at height; penetration speed at low altitude is about 405 mph (625 km/h). The B-52A entered service in August 1954; subsequently 744 aircraft were built in eight major types, culminating in the B-52H — essentially a B-52G with the TF33 turbofan and M61 six-barrel tail cannon

Below *Conceived For Liberty*, a B-52G-100-W of the 93rd Bombardment Wing, carried this Bald Eagle marking in August 1984. The nose radome is hinged upwards so as to allow access to the digital and hardened nav/bombing system, which is capable of precision fixing and weapon delivery down to 300 ft. Complete revision of the navigation and weapon-training suite of the B-52G/H under the $1.6 billion Offensive Avionics System programme was completed in 1987

Crew bus in the background, a B-52G is pre-flighted before a scheduled training mission. The B-52G was the most numerous variant, 193 being delivered from early 1959

Left Boeing meets Boeing: a B-52H tops up from a KC-135 tanker of the Utah Air National Guard. The range of the Strato-fortress is unlimited with air refuelling suport; even without this, the B-52H is capable of flying 10,130 miles (16,303 km). Displayed for the benefit of Joe Cupido's camera are the windows for the Electro-optical Viewing System (EVS). When not in use, the twin steerable turrets under the nose are

normally rotated 180° to prevent the accumulation of airborne particles from degrading the sensors associated with the Hughes AN/AAQ-6 forward-looking infrared (FLIR), and Westinghouse AN/AVQ-22 steerable TV (STV)—system. Both the G and H were retrofitted with EVS equipment in the early 1970s

Below A B-52G running in with its bomb doors open – a sight guaranteed to chill the heart of an enemy. No G model is less than 30 years old, but as Saddam Hussein's so-called elite Republican Guard discovered in Desert Storm, its bomb-load is devastating. The main conventional B-52 force comprises 68 G models which were never modified to carry ALCMs. These BUFFs can carry 51 weapons in the Mk 82 500 lb class – 27 internally and 24 on wing pylons – or 18 Mk 84 2000 lb bombs. Precision-guided munitions may also be carried; eg eight Rafael/Martin-Marietta AGM-142As. This rocket-powered ASM is equipped with a 700 lb warhead and has a range of 110 km. The missile guides itself towards its target and, when in range, transmits an imaging infrared (IIR) view of the target to the B-52. The radar navigator selects an aim-point on the target, and the missile's IIR seeker guides it to impact

The B-52G introduced a 'wet' wing which increased internal fuel from 35,550 to 46,575 US gal. Both the G and H feature roll control by spoilers only, evidenced here as this BUFF holds station behind a KC-135 tanker

With landing and taxi lights switched on to make the aircraft as visible as possible to other traffic, a BUFF returns to Tinker AFB as day turns to night

Key penetration aids applied to the B-52G/H fleet included the installation of Phase VI ECM equipment and a subsequent update programme which culminated with the ITT Avionics ALQ-172 Pave Mint ECM system which, ironically, proved to be far superior to the defensive avionics fit of the B-1B. Bomb-doors open, a B-52G of the 416th BW stokes up its eight J57s for a fast low-level run over the target

Decorated with a 'low-vis' Statue of Liberty on the tail, a B-52G of the 668th Bombardment Squadron, 416th Bombardment Wing, approaches its home base at Griffiss AFB in upstate New York. Just visible is the G model's defensive tail sting – four .50 calibre M3 machine guns

Lancer

Above A B-1B with the wings swept back. They pivot from 15° (leading-edge angle) to 67.5°. This big range of sweep makes an enormous difference to the Lancer's ability to match shape to different demands, even though the original requirement to fly at Mach 2 at high altitude was abandoned. In the Tu-160 the Mach number at high altitude can exceed 1.9, but the B-1B is not intended for more than 1.25. Today even a modest amount of 'stealth' capability is worth much more than extra speed, and in any case you cannot fly very fast at low level

Left Air refuelling receptacle open, a Rockwell B-1B Lancer noses in under the tail of the tanker. The sombre dark finish – often looking like dark charcoal grey but actually a grey and two shades of dark green – is relieved only by the pattern of white bars above the nose. These are foot-markers to help the refuelling boomer judge distance

Overleaf The B-1B is an in-between aircraft, generations later than the B-52 and incorporating areas of RAM (radar-absorbent materials) skinning, yet a generation earlier than the Soviet Tu-160, which is much larger and 84 per cent more powerful yet with markedly smaller RCS (radar cross-section). RCS of any swing-wing aircraft varies with wing sweep angle, but the value for the B-1B is certainly less than one-quarter that for a B-52. The USAF claims it to be only one-hundredth as great

Left B-1B crews routinely practice air refuelling, from both KC-135R and KC-10A aircraft; here the tanker is a 135. The bomber can carry 195,000 lb of fuel, not including extra bladders which can be carried in the weapon bays, either to extend range beyond the brochure figure of 12,000 km (7457 miles) or as ballast

Right Practice interceptions may or may not be representative of what might happen in any future war, but they are good training for bomber crews and fighter pilots alike. Here an F-16B from the 184th Tactical Fighter Group, Kansas Air National Guard, pulls up beside a B-1B from the 384th Bomb Wing. Both are out of McConnell AFB, at Wichita

Preceding pages Externally, apart from the colour, the B-1B looks very much like the B-1A prototypes flown from 1974. Internally they are quite different aircraft. The whole airframe had to be redesigned to withstand the stresses of flight at low level, and at weights increased from 389,000 lb to 477,000 lb. The engine inlets were greatly simplified, variable geometry features being replaced by baffles to screen the engines from enemy radars. The ejectable crew capsule was replaced by four conventional ejection seats. And the whole aircraft was stuffed with complex defensive electronics systems — which, in fact, have caused more trouble than everything else combined

Below *Wichita Express* flies with the 384th Bombardment Wing (Heavy), whose 28th Bombardment Squadron was the sixth and last to be equipped with the B-1B. In this view the small downsloping foreplanes can be seen, looking from the front like a waxed moustache. They are driven by the SMCS (structural mode control system) to damp out response to flight through low-level turbulence, which would otherwise not only eat rapidly into fatigue life but also 'shake the crew's eyeballs out'

Head-on the Lancer shows that the redesigned engine pods curve in sharply at the top. Between them there is not much room for the massive main gears, which accordingly fold away to the rear, and slightly inwards. With the giant slats at 20°, where an F-111 is red, a Lancer is white. And the whole forward-facing area of the fuselage and wing roots is in reality a series of avionics antennas

Below Flying the B-1B is fine, but there are times when you have to be accurate. One is on landing, when you have to hold the wings level. As this taxiing shot emphasizes, the span with the wings at 15° is considerable, the tips are quite near the ground and the track of the main gears is narrow. This was one of the first aircraft, with very prominent air-refuelling markings and white-outlined foreplanes

Below right Taxiing past, this early Lancer shows the unpainted flexible strips which seal the compartment above the engines into which the trailing edge of the wing retracts as sweep angle increases. Of course, the flaps have to be fully housed first. The shadow shows how the Sun can shine through the gap ahead of the extended flaps

Right Externally there is no evidence of the mass of avionics at the tail. The defensive system receiving antennas are at the top of the fin. The main radar warning antennas are in the aft end of the fin/tailplane bullet fairing. The large group of defensive system transmitting antennas fill the tail end of the fuselage. Prolonged difficulties with the giant ALQ-161 defensive avionics system resulted in cancellation of the entire 161A system in March 1991. The Air Force said 'Revisions . . . could not overcome the basic design flaws.' This is having a profound (hopefully temporary) effect on the B-1B's ability to fly its missions

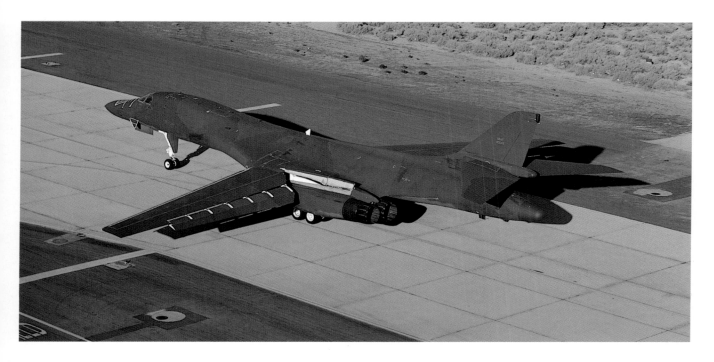

Right Every B-1B base contains hundreds of millions of dollars' worth of 'yellow stuff' (ground support equipment), much of it specially tailored to the aircraft. Here routine line maintenance is in progress on the main radar. This, the Westinghouse APQ-164, is a multi-mode set with a phased-array flat antenna made up of 1526 separate transmitting antennas. Amazingly, much of this radar was based on the small set fitted to the F-16

Below Each B-1B is powered by four General Electric F101-102 augmented turbofans, each rated at 17,000 lb in military thrust and 'in the 30,000 lb class' (unofficially said to be 29,600) with full 'burner. The F118, a development of the same engine but without afterburner, powers the B-2. In the B-2 far greater efforts have been made to reduce infrared and aural signatures

Right This Lancer, seen here with its spoilers/lift dumpers open, is assigned as a permanent flying test bed for all modifications to be made to aircraft in service with SAC bomb wings. It is based at Edwards AFB, the Air Force Flight Test Center

Below Every Lancer base has all the necessary electrical, pneumatic and air-conditioning supplies routed underneath the apron to emerge at every parking spot. Thus, soon after each aircraft has returned from each mission it appears to be in the grip of some malevolent octopus. The motto of the 96th at Dyess (first B-1B base) is *E Sempre l'Ora,* or 'It's always the hour'

Below right Not only nose art but the names of the flight and ground crews adorn every aircraft in line service. More than that, the name (and usually nose art) is repeated on ground equipment such as this equipment at Dyess AFB, home of the 96th Bomb Wing. It even extends to individual tool boxes

Below Standard munitions loaders are familiar throughout the USAF, but the B-1B needs something else. Called the Type 196 Loader, it can put loads into a B-1B with an individual weight of 88,000 lb. Indeed, an Air Force release gives the maximum bombload as 125,000 lb. Here a CSRL (common strategic rotary launcher) is about to go aboard, carrying four B83 nuclear weapons (of which a B-1B can carry 14)

Left This gives some idea of the size and complexity of the 196 loader. It takes about half an hour to load each of the three internal bays, or 90 minutes to fill the interior completely. If AGM-86B (later AGM-129A) cruise missiles are to be carried they go in Bay 2, with the dividing bulkhead moved forward to leave a small forward bay for a fuel cell. SRAMs (AGM-69 or 131) can go in the aft bay, and there are also eight external stores stations

Right This CSRL was loaded into the middle of the three internal weapon bays, all of which have two similar hydraulically actuated doors. The B83 is only 12 ft long, about 2 in longer than the numerous B61, whereas the maximum available length of the combined two forward bays is 31 ft 3 in. Each CSRL can be loaded with eight weapons, dropped in any desired sequence

Overleaf No aircraft in history – not even Britain's TSR.2 – has been subjected to such sustained and mindless vitriol from its own media as the B-1B Lancer. Fortunately for the United States the unthinking knockers did not win, and this bomber – unlike the TSR.2 – has survived to play the central role in the deterrent force of USAF Strategic Air Command. If you want to find out what the B-1B is really like, don't try the newspapers or TV – ask the crews who fly it

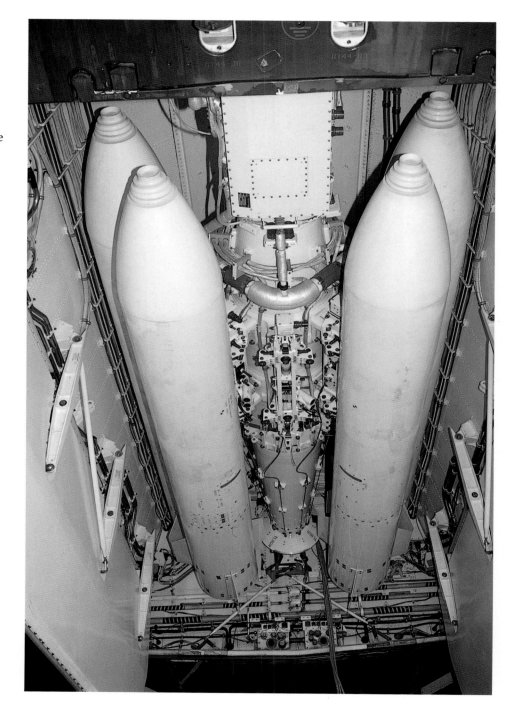